Piano • Vocal • Guitar

THE GREATEST SONGS
of the
LAST CENTURY

THE CHOICE OF SONGS

Any list of the top songs from 100 years of music reflects only one point of view, of course. In an era so musically rich and varied, the real challenge lies not so much in deciding which songs to include, but which ones *not* to include.

There are many "classic" twentieth century songs that have successfully stood the test of time, but there are also songs written near the close of the century with the same enduring qualities. The editors of this publication have attempted to choose a collection of songs that is worthy to represent the last century as a whole.

When the choices became difficult, it was the craft of songwriting that tipped the scales in a song's favor, over recorded performance. We also were aware of representing different genres and periods of twentieth century popular song—Broadway, jazz standards, rock era standards, classic country and movie songs are all to be found here. Surely among our choices are some of your very favorite songs.

Here's to a century of memories.

—The Editors

ISBN 0-634-02118-4

HAL•LEONARD®
CORPORATION

7777 W. BLUEMOUND RD. P.O. BOX 13819 MILWAUKEE, WI 53213

Visit Hal Leonard Online at
www.halleonard.com

THE GREATEST SONGS of the LAST CENTURY

TABLE OF CONTENTS

ALFIE
Theme from the Paramount Picture ALFIE

Words by HAL DAVID
Music by BURT BACHARACH

Very Slowly, Rubato

ALL I ASK OF YOU

from THE PHANTOM OF THE OPERA

Music by ANDREW LLOYD WEBBER
Lyrics by CHARLES HART
Additional Lyrics by RICHARD STILGOE

ALWAYS ON MY MIND

Words and Music by WAYNE THOMPSON,
MARK JAMES and JOHNNY CHRISTOPHER

ANGEL

Words and Music by
SARAH McLACHLAN

Original key: D♭ major. This edition has been transposed down one half-step to be more playable.

BEAUTY AND THE BEAST
from Walt Disney's BEAUTY AND THE BEAST

Lyrics by HOWARD ASHMAN
Music by ALAN MENKEN

Tale as old as time, true as it can be. Bare-ly e-ven friends, then some-bod-y bends un-ex-pect-ed-

BÉSAME MUCHO
(Kiss Me Much)

Music and Spanish Words by
CONSUELO VELAZQUEZ
English Words by SUNNY SKYLAR

Bé - sa - me, _____ bé - sa - me mu - cho, _____
Bé - sa - me, _____ bé - sa - me mu - cho, _____

each time I cling to your kiss I hear mu - sic di - vine. _____
co - mo si fue - ra es - ta no - che la úl - ti - ma vez; _____

Bé - sa - me mu - cho, _____
bé - sa - me mu - cho, _____

BOHEMIAN RHAPSODY

from HIGH SCHOOL HIGH

Words and Music by
FREDDIE MERCURY

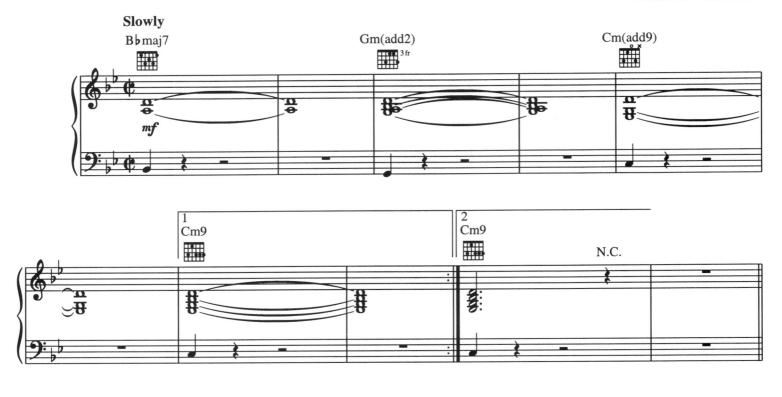

Ma - ma ___ just killed a man, ___ put a
Too late, ___ my time has come. ___ Sends

gun a - gainst ___ his head, ___ pulled my trig - ger. Now, ___ he's dead. ___
shiv - ers down ___ my spine. ___ Bod - y's ach - ing all ___ the time. ___

CABARET
from the Musical CABARET

Words by FRED EBB
Music by JOHN KANDER

BRAZIL

Words and Music by S.K. RUSSELL
and ARY BARROSO

CAN YOU FEEL THE LOVE TONIGHT

(Pop Version)

from Walt Disney's THE LION KING
As Performed by Elton John

Music by ELTON JOHN
Lyrics by TIM RICE

CHANGE THE WORLD

featured on the Motion Picture Soundtrack PHENOMENON

Words and Music by WAYNE KIRKPATRICK,
GORDON KENNEDY and TOMMY SIMS

54

CRY ME A RIVER

Words and Music by
ARTHUR HAMILTON

Now _____ you say you're lone-ly, _____

You cry the long night thru, _____ well, you can cry _____ me a riv - er,

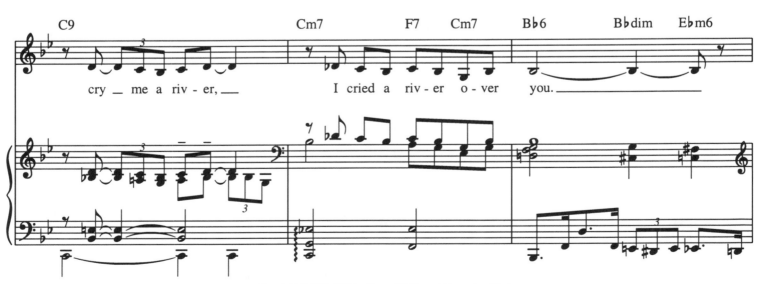

cry ___ me a riv - er, ___ I cried a riv - er o - ver you. _____

CRYING

Words and Music by ROY ORBISON
and JOE MELSON

wished me well; ___ you could-n't tell _____ that I'd been
don't love me and I'll al-ways be _____

cry - ing o - ver you, cry - ing
cry - ing o - ver you, cry - ing

o - ver you. When you said, "So
o - ver you. Yes, now you're ___

long;" left me stand-ing _____ all a - lone, a - lone and
gone and from this _____ mo-ment on I'll be

A DAY IN THE LIFE OF A FOOL
(Manha De Carnaval)

Words by CARL SIGMAN
Music by LUIZ BONFA

Slow Bossa Nova

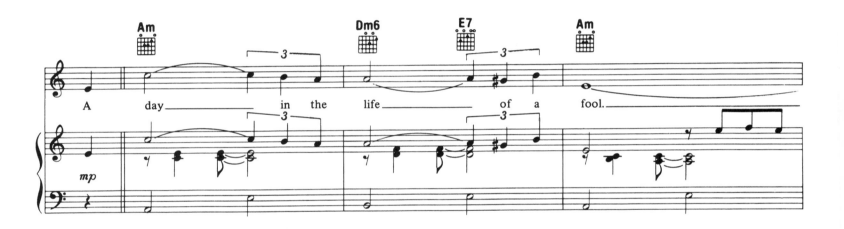

ELEANOR RIGBY

Words and Music by JOHN LENNON
and PAUL McCARTNEY

Moderately, with a steady beat

Ah_____ look at all____ the lone - ly peo - ple!_____

Ah_____ look at all____ the lone - ly peo -

- ple!_____

El - ea - nor Rig - by,
Fa - ther Mc Ken - zie
El - ea - nor Rig - by,

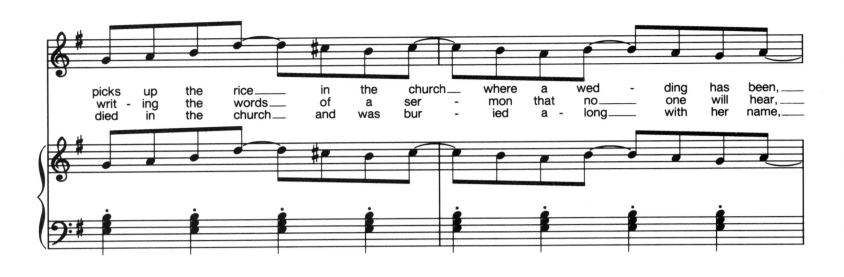

picks up the rice___ in the church___ where a wed - ding has been,___
writ - ing the words___ of a ser - mon that no___ one will hear,___
died in the church___ and was bur - ied a - long___ with her name,___

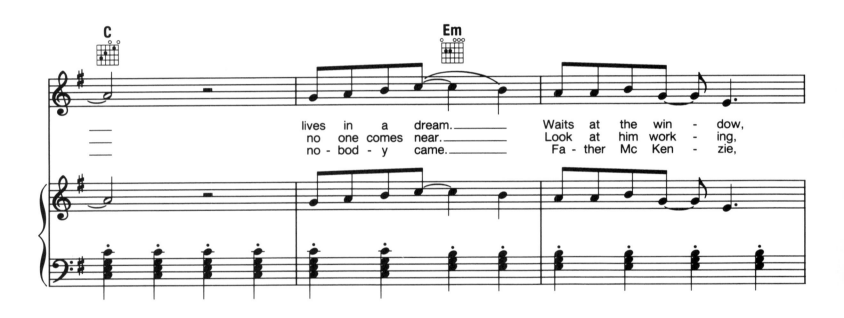

C   Em

___ lives in a dream.___ Waits at the win - dow,
___ no one comes near.___ Look at him work - ing,
___ no - bod - y came.___ Fa - ther Mc Ken - zie,

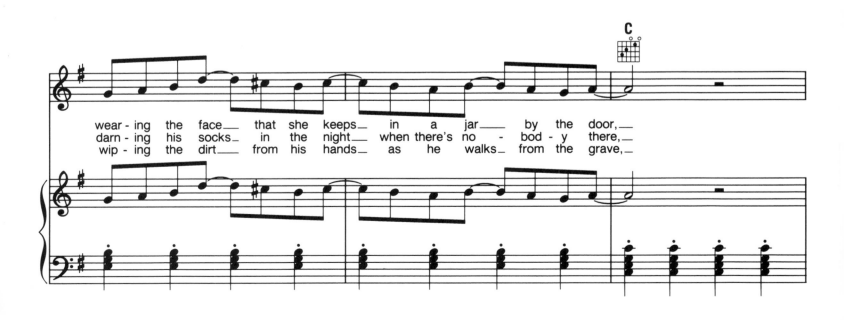

C

wear - ing the face___ that she keeps___ in a jar___ by the door,___
darn - ing his socks___ in the night___ when there's no - bod - y there,___
wip - ing the dirt___ from his hands___ as he walks___ from the grave,___

DUST IN THE WIND

Words and Music by
KERRY LIVGREN

EASTER PARADE

featured in the Motion Picture Irving Berlin's EASTER PARADE
from AS THOUSANDS CHEER

Words and Music by
IRVING BERLIN

ENDLESS LOVE
from ENDLESS LOVE

Words and Music by
LIONEL RICHIE

FIRE AND RAIN

Words and Music by
JAMES TAYLOR

Verse 3:

walk-ing my mind to an eas-y time my back turned towards the sun

Lord knows when the cold wind blows it -'ll turn your head_ a -round___ Well, there's

hours of time_ on the tel - e -phone line_ to talk a -bout things to come___

Sweet dreams and fly - ing ma - chines in pie - ces on_____ the ground.

FOR ONCE IN MY LIFE

Words by RONALD MILLER
Music by ORLANDO MURDEN

FIELDS OF GOLD

Written and Composed by
STING

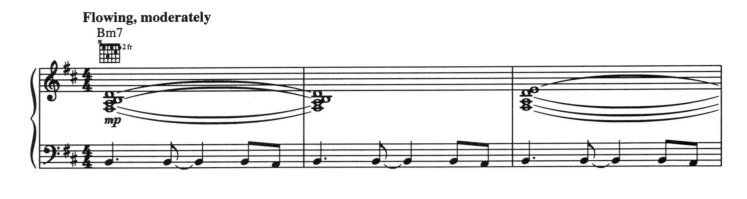

Flowing, moderately

You'll re - mem - ber me, when the west wind moves _ up -
stay with me, will you be my love _ a -

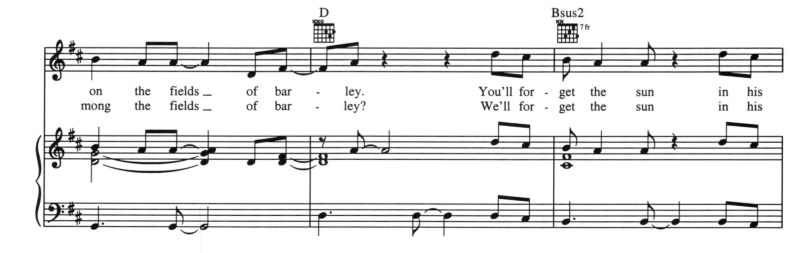

on the fields _ of bar - ley. You'll for - get the sun in his
mong the fields _ of bar - ley? We'll for - get the sun in his

GREAT BALLS OF FIRE

Words and Music by OTIS BLACKWELL
and JACK HAMMER

so kind, __ I'm gon-na tell the world that you're mine, mine, mine, mine. __

I chew my nails and I twid-dle my thumb. __ I'm real ner-vous but it

sure is fun. __ Come on, ba-by, you're driv-ing me cra-zy. Good-ness gra-cious, great __

__ balls of fire! Good-ness gra-cious, great __ balls of fire!

GEORGIA ON MY MIND

Words by STUART GORRELL
Music by HOAGY CARMICHAEL

GOD BLESS' THE CHILD

featured in the Motion Picture LADY SINGS THE BLUES
from BUBBLING BROWN SUGAR

Words and Music by ARTHUR HERZOG JR.
and BILLIE HOLIDAY

GROW OLD WITH ME

Words and Music by
JOHN LENNON

HELLO, DOLLY!
from HELLO, DOLLY!

Music and Lyric by
JERRY HERMAN

HEY JUDE

Words and Music by JOHN LENNON
and PAUL McCARTNEY

I HEARD IT THROUGH THE GRAPEVINE

Words and Music by NORMAN J. WHITFIELD
and BARRETT STRONG

D.S. al Coda

Peo - ple say be - lieve half _

CODA,

_ yeah, yeah, _ yeah. I heard it through the grape - vine, not much

Repeat and Fade

lon - ger would you be mine, ba - by. Yeah, _

I LEFT MY HEART IN
SAN FRANCISCO

Words by DOUGLASS CROSS
Music by GEORGE CORY

I SAY A LITTLE PRAYER

featured in the TriStar Motion Picture MY BEST FRIEND'S WEDDING

Lyric by HAL DAVID
Music by BURT BACHARACH

(1.) The mo - ment I wake up,
(2.) I run ___ for the bus, dear.
(D.S.) *Instrumental solo*

be - fore ___ I put on my make - up,
While rid - ing, I think of us, dear.

I
(I

Gmaj7   Am7/D   Gmaj7

prayer. Say you love me, too.

Am7/D

Gmaj7

Why don't you an - swer my prayer?

Am7/D

Repeat and Fade

You know, ev - 'ry day I say a lit - tle

I WILL REMEMBER YOU

Theme from THE BROTHERS McMULLEN

Words and Music by SARAH McLACHLAN,
SEAMUS EGAN and DAVE MERENDA

IF EVER I WOULD LEAVE YOU
from CAMELOT

Words by ALAN JAY LERNER
Music by FREDERICK LOEWE

Intro: Moderately

I'VE GROWN ACCUSTOMED TO HER FACE

from MY FAIR LADY

Words by ALAN JAY LERNER
Music by FREDERICK LOEWE

IF I LOVED YOU
from CAROUSEL

Lyrics by OSCAR HAMMERSTEIN II
Music by RICHARD RODGERS

Allegretto moderato

IMAGINE

Words and Music by
JOHN LENNON

Slowly

I-mag-ine there's no heav-en. ___

It's eas-y if you ___ try. ___ No hell ___ be-low us, ___

___ a-bove us on-ly sky. ___

THE IMPOSSIBLE DREAM
(The Quest)
from MAN OF LA MANCHA

Lyric by JOE DARION
Music by MITCH LEIGH

152

IN MY LIFE

Words and Music by JOHN LENNON
and PAUL McCARTNEY

IN THE STILL OF THE NIGHT

from NIGHT AND DAY

Words and Music by
COLE PORTER

160

IT'S IMPOSSIBLE
(Somos Novios)

English Lyric by SID WAYNE
Spanish Words and Music by
ARMANDO MANZANERO

Slowly, with expression

Lyrics:

It's im-pos-si-ble, tell the
So-mos no-vios

sun to leave the sky, it's just im-pos-si-ble.
dos sen-ti-mos mu tuo a-mor pro-fun-do

It's im-pos-si-ble, ask a
Y con e-so ya ga-

KING OF THE ROAD

Words and Music by
ROGER MILLER

Trail-er for sale or rent, rooms to let fif-ty cents.
Third box-car mid-night train, des-ti-na-tion: Ban-gor, Maine.

No phone, no pool, no pets; I ain't got no cig-a-rettes..Ah, but
Old worn-out suit and shoes; I don't pay no un-ion dues. I smoke

two hours of push-ing broom buys a eight by twelve four bit room.I'm a
old sto-gies I have found, short but not too big a-round.I'm a

man of means ___ by no means, king of the road. ___

I know ev-er-y en-gi-neer on ev-er-y train, ___ all of the chil-dren and

all of their names, ___ and ev-er-y hand-out in ev-er-y town, ___ and

ev'-ry lock that ain't locked when no one's a-round. ___ I sing

JAILHOUSE ROCK

featured in the Motion Picture THE BLUES BROTHERS
from SMOKEY JOE'S CAFE

Words and Music by JERRY LEIBER
and MIKE STOLLER

1. The war-den threw a par-ty in the
2.-5. *(See additional lyrics)*

coun-ty jail. ___ The pris-on band was there and they be-

gan to wail. The band was jump-in' and the joint be-

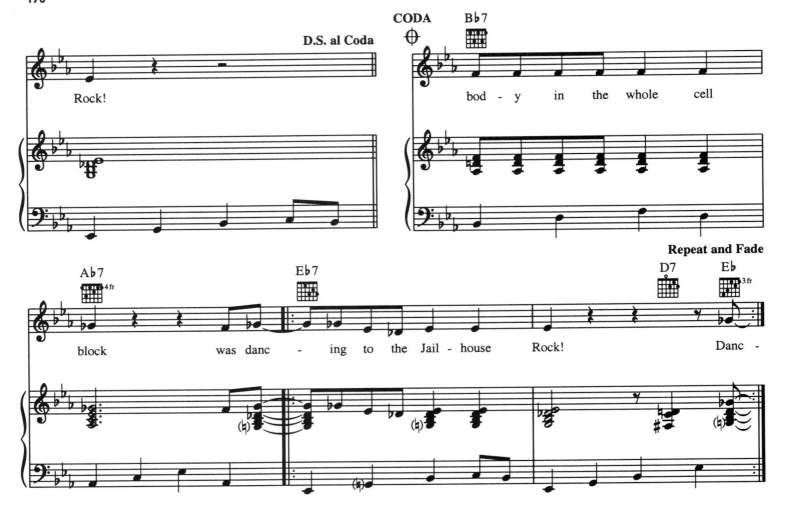

Additional Lyrics

2. Spider Murphy played the tenor saxophone
   Little Joe was blowin' on the slide trombone.
   The drummer boy from Illinois went crash, boon, bang;
   The whole rhythm section was the Purple Gang.
   (Chorus)

3. Number Forty-seven said to number Three:
   "You're the cutest jailbird I ever did see.
   I sure would be delighted with your company,
   Come on and do the Jailhouse Rock with me."
   (Chorus)

4. The sad sack was a-sittin' on a block of stone,
   Way over in the corner weeping all alone.
   The warden said: "Hey, Buddy, don't you be no square,
   If you can't find a partner, use a wooden chair!"
   (Chorus)

5. Shifty Henry said to Bugs: "For heaven's sake,
   No one's lookin', now's our chance to make a break."
   Bugsy turned to Shifty and he said: "Nix, nix;
   I wanna stick around a while and get my kicks."
   (Chorus)

JUST THE WAY YOU ARE

Words and Music by
BILLY JOEL

KILLING ME SOFTLY WITH HIS SONG

Words by NORMAN GIMBEL
Music by CHARLES FOX

MEMORY
from CATS

Music by ANDREW LLOYD WEBBER
Text by TREVOR NUNN after T.S. ELIOT

MISTY

Words by JOHNNY BURKE
Music by ERROLL GARNER

MOON RIVER

from the Paramount Picture BREAKFAST AT TIFFANY'S

Words by JOHNNY MERCER
Music by HENRY MANCINI

MY CHERIE AMOUR

Words and Music by STEVIE WONDER,
SYLVIA MOY and HENRY COSBY

MY FUNNY VALENTINE
from BABES IN ARMS

Words by LORENZ HART
Music by RICHARD RODGERS

MY GIRL

featured in the Motion Picture MY GIRL

Words and Music by WILLIAM "SMOKEY" ROBINSON
and RONALD WHITE

THE RAINBOW CONNECTION
from THE MUPPET MOVIE

By PAUL WILLIAMS
and KENNETH L. ASCHER

MY HEART WILL GO ON
(Love Theme from 'Titanic')
from the Paramount and Twentieth Century Fox Motion Picture TITANIC

Music by JAMES HORNER
Lyric by WILL JENNINGS

Ev - 'ry night in my dreams I see you, I feel you, that is how I know you go on.

ONE FOR MY BABY
(And One More for the Road)
from the Motion Picture THE SKY'S THE LIMIT

Lyric by JOHNNY MERCER
Music by HAROLD ARLEN

PEOPLE
from FUNNY GIRL

Words by BOB MERRILL
Music by JULE STYNE

PUTTIN' ON THE RITZ
from the Motion Picture PUTTIN' ON THE RITZ

Words and Music by
IRVING BERLIN

SEPTEMBER SONG
from the Musical Play KNICKERBOCKER HOLIDAY

Words by MAXWELL ANDERSON
Music by KURT WEILL

RAINDROPS KEEP FALLIN' ON MY HEAD

from BUTCH CASSIDY AND THE SUNDANCE KID

Lyric by HAL DAVID
Music by BURT BACHARACH

SATIN DOLL
from SOPHISTICATED LADIES

Words by JOHNNY MERCER and BILLY STRAYHORN
Music by DUKE ELLINGTON

SKYLARK

Words by JOHNNY MERCER
Music by HOAGY CARMICHAEL

SOMETHING

Words and Music by
GEORGE HARRISON

Some - thing in ____ the way ____ she moves, _
Some - where in ____ her smile ____ she knows, _
Some - thing in ____ the way ____ she knows, _

at - tracts _ me like _ no oth-er lov - er.
that I ____ don't need _ no oth-er lov - er.
and all ____ I have _ to do is think _ of her.

Some-thing in _ the way _ she woos _____ me. _
Some-thing in _ her style _ that shows _____ me. _
Some-thing in _ the things _ she shows _____ me. _

I don't want to leave _ her now,   you

SOPHISTICATED LADY

Words and Music by DUKE ELLINGTON,
IRVING MILLS and MITCHELL PARISH

STAND BY ME
featured in the Motion Picture STAND BY ME

Words and Music by BEN E. KING,
JERRY LEIBER and MIKE STOLLER

STAR DUST

Words by MITCHELL PARISH
Music by HOAGY CARMICHAEL

Moderately

...And now the pur-ple dusk of twi-light time

steals a-cross the mead-ows of my heart.

High up in the sky the

lit-tle stars climb,

al-ways re-mind-ing me that

STAYIN' ALIVE
from SATURDAY NIGHT FEVER

Words and Music by BARRY GIBB,
MAURICE GIBB and ROBIN GIBB

Fm7

Some-bod - y help me. ___ Some-bod - y help_me, yeah. ___

Bb7

Life go - in' no where. ___ Some-bod - y help_ me, yeah. ___

Fm7

D.S. al Coda (lyric 1)

Stay-in' a - live. ___ Well, you can tell_

CODA **Fm7** **Bb7**

Life go - in' no - where. ___

STORMY WEATHER
(Keeps Rainin' All the Time)

from COTTON CLUB PARADE OF 1933
featured in the Motion Picture STORMY WEATHER

Lyric by TED KOEHLER
Music by HAROLD ARLEN

Interlude

TAKE THE "A" TRAIN

Words and Music by
BILLY STRAYHORN

TEARS IN HEAVEN

featured in the Motion Picture RUSH

Words and Music by ERIC CLAPTON
and WILL JENNINGS

Be-yond   the door ____   there's peace, I'm sure, _

THERE'S NO BUSINESS LIKE SHOW BUSINESS

from the Stage Production ANNIE GET YOUR GUN

Words and Music by
IRVING BERLIN

TIME IN A BOTTLE

Words and Music by
JIM CROCE

UNCHAINED MELODY

from the Motion Picture UNCHAINED
featured in the Motion Picture GHOST

Lyric by HY ZARET
Music by ALEX NORTH

A WHITER SHADE OF PALE

Words and Music by KEITH REID
and GARY BROOKER

WHAT A WONDERFUL WORLD

featured in the Motion Picture GOOD MORNING VIETNAM

Words and Music by GEORGE DAVID WEISS
and BOB THIELE

WONDERFUL TONIGHT

Words and Music by
ERIC CLAPTON

It's late in the eve - ning;
We go to a par - ty,
It's time to go home __ now,

she's won-d'ring what clothes __ to wear. __
and ev - 'ry - one turns __ to see __
and I've got an ach - ing head. __

She puts on her make -
this beau - ti - ful la -
So I give her the car __

I feel won-der-ful ____ be-cause I see ____ the love ____ light in ____ your eyes. Then the won-der of it all ____ is that you just don't ____ re-al-ize ____ how much ____ I love ____ you.

YESTERDAY

Words and Music by JOHN LENNON
and PAUL McCARTNEY

Moderately, with expression

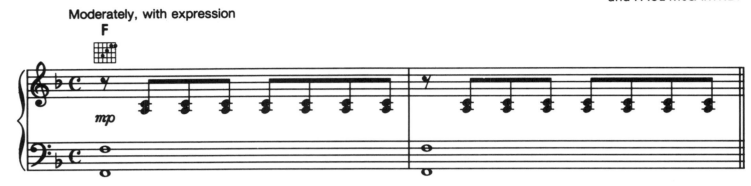

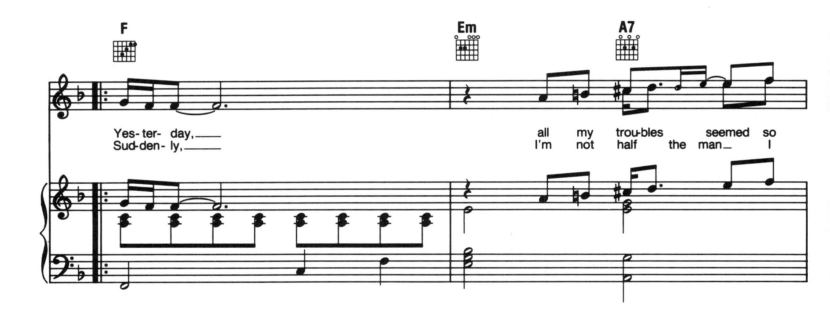

Yes-ter- day,____ all my trou-bles seemed so
Sud-den- ly,____ I'm not half the man__ I

far a - way;____ Now it looks as though_ they're
used to be, There's a sha - dow hang - ing

YOU'LL NEVER WALK ALONE
from CAROUSEL

Lyrics by OSCAR HAMMERSTEIN II
Music by RICHARD RODGERS

* alternate lyric: hold your head up high

YOUR CHEATIN' HEART

Words and Music by
HANK WILLIAMS